Dad's Journal to Financial Freedom

By LC Hancock

Dad's Journal to Financial Freedom

© 2025 LC Hancock

All rights reserved. No part of this book may be reproduced, stored in a retrieval system, or transmitted in any form or by any means—electronic, mechanical, photocopying, recording, or otherwise—without prior written permission of the author, except in the case of brief quotations used in reviews, articles, or academic works.

This book is a work of nonfiction. The events, experiences, and opinions expressed are based on the author's life and personal perspective. Any resemblance to actual persons or organizations is coincidental unless specifically noted.

Published by Independently Published

ISBN (paperback): 979-8-9931980-1-9

Disclaimer

The information in this book is provided for educational and informational purposes only. It should not be construed as financial, investment, tax, legal, or accounting advice. The author is not a licensed financial advisor, broker, dealer, tax professional, or attorney, and nothing here should be relied on as a substitute for advice from a qualified professional.

All examples, scenarios, case studies, and strategies are illustrative only and do not constitute specific recommendations. Any references to investments, securities, businesses, or financial instruments are provided solely for discussion and should not be interpreted as endorsements or solicitations.

Readers are solely responsible for their own financial decisions. The author and publisher make no representations or warranties, express or implied, regarding the accuracy, completeness, or suitability of the information. No guarantee of financial outcomes is made or implied.

The author and publisher expressly disclaim all liability for any direct, indirect, incidental, consequential, or other damages arising from the use of, reliance on, or application of the information in this book. By reading further, you acknowledge and agree that you are acting solely at your own risk.

Table of Contents

Chapter 1: The Nine Circles of Education 1

Chapter 2: Wolf in Sheep's Clothing 5

Chapter 3: Blue or Red Pill 9

Chapter 4: Exodus 14

Chapter 5: Breakthrough 18

Chapter 6: Philosophy of Money 23

Chapter 7: Reflection 33

LC Hancock

Introduction

This book was previously released under the title ***Poor Dad's Diary to Graduating Poverty University***.

This book is a collection of my mistakes and successes over the years—written for my children and everybody. My aim is to guide, to bring awareness, to help you avoid pitfalls, and to give you tools to navigate life's challenges in pursuit of financial freedom.

There are valuable lessons I've learned that I wish I had discovered earlier. I wish someone had pushed me onto the path of financial education in my youth. My hope is to help you begin building your wealth. I've made the mistakes so that you don't have to.

Chapter 1: The Nine Circles of Education

My parents brought us to the United States in 1992 as a result of the Vietnam War. As first-generation immigrants, we started from nothing and like many families, we didn't have much money growing up. Being the oldest of eight children came with heavy responsibilities. We lived paycheck to paycheck, often relying on government programs for essentials.

In pursuit of a better life, my parents constantly reinforced the idea that we must study hard, get good grades, graduate high school, go to college, earn a degree, and secure a well-paying job. This was programmed into me by my parents and elders long before school could. School merely reminded me to stay on that path.

We have a saying that roughly translates to: "One day, I'll still eat without doing; with little effort, I will have enough." My parents reminded me that education was the key to escaping poverty and achieving a more comfortable life than they had. A desk job—a position of power requiring only the use of my mind and pen—was seen as success. Leadership roles were praised by family and community, the higher the degree, the more prestigious it was. News of such accomplishments would spread like wildfire through relatives, elevating one's social standing and even marriage prospects.

In school, teachers often told us, "Pay attention, because you never know when you might need this in life." Yet none of those lessons were about money. We all learned later, in the real world, that money is what we needed—and often a lot of it. The closest subject to finance was mathematics. Other subjects provided enough knowledge for small talks. There is a vast difference between being academically smart and being financially smart.

I recommend Robert Kiyosaki's *Why "A" Students Work for "C" Students and "B" Students Work for the Government.* Many avoid discussing money because it makes people uncomfortable—perhaps because it forces them to question their reality: the grind of schooling, job, pay raises, and climbing the corporate ladder. This is called the "rat race." Schools prepare us to be employees, not entrepreneurs. They teach us to show up on time, follow instructions, and produce good results. Fail at these, and you're penalized; fail enough times at your job, and you're fired.

School teaches you how to be a consumer, not how to build wealth. If everyone learned wealth-building, there would be a shortage of employees, not a shortage of jobs. Who would flip hamburgers if everyone were financially independent?

By my senior year in 2007, I already had enough credits to graduate but still attended full-time, taking electives. One was Personal Finance. At the time, smartphones and investment apps didn't exist. To invest in the stock market, you had to go through traditional brokers. My young mind struggled to understand the stock market, dividends, and even basic concepts like checking accounts and interest.

The course was only one quarter long—not nearly enough to grasp finance. If money management had been taught consistently like other subjects, students would graduate with a strong foundation. Still, it gave me exposure. Our teacher taught from textbooks, and once or twice a week we had a guest speaker named Jeff. He was an older man, retired early, living off his investments. He spoke about stocks and dividends, most of which went over my head.

I remember Jeff sharing a story about a student that asked him: "What if we save and invest our money, but die before we can use it?" Jeff cleverly replied: "If you don't save or invest, when you really need that money, you'll wish you were dead." Looking back, I think Jeff wanted to say more but treaded carefully. After all, schools aren't in the business of producing entrepreneurs. I don't recall learning about cash flow or passive income—only the tip of the iceberg.

I graduated with about a 3.0 GPA and moved on to the next chapter: college. "Go to college, get a degree, and you'll get a good job," my parents said. So I enrolled in ITT Tech to study Criminal Justice. I didn't realize it was a private college and ended up graduating in 2011 with nearly $100,000 in student debt.

At the time, I didn't know that the average cost for the same degree could be $20,000–$30,000—or that skipping college altogether might have been wiser. My parents only cared that I was going, not what it cost. Years later, ITT Tech was shut down for legal reasons. My degree now sits in a vault, unused. If you went to college and ended up in a different field, you're not alone.

I still remember the phone ringing every morning with lenders demanding their student loan payment. Every time I applied for a loan—for a car or a house—the $100,000 debt worked against me. Even with a credit score in the mid-to-high 700s, it didn't matter; my debt-to-income ratio (DTI) was too high. I often needed a co-signer. If you're unsure about your career path, I advise you to hold off on college. Debt-free is better than a useless degree.

As I later learned, you don't need a degree to build wealth. You need financial education. Many people with PhDs still struggle with money, while others without degrees earn millions through creativity. A six-figure salary doesn't guarantee freedom if you lack financial literacy.

At that time, I preached to my younger siblings that adulthood required three things as a starter kit: a driver's license, a job, and a credit score. A license offers independence, a job provided income and good credit leads to leverage.

A credit score of 680 is considered good; 700+ is stronger. Without a credit history, banks won't issue you a credit card. That's where secured credit cards come in—you deposit your own money (say $300) and use it like a credit line. After six months of responsible use, you build history, and banks will start sending offers.

Credit cards can be powerful tools if used wisely. Treat them like debit cards: never spend more than you have, and pay the balance in full before the end of your billing cycle to avoid the high interest rates of 18–

30%. A $10 sandwich charged on credit could cost much more if you carry the balance. Discipline is key—credit can be a lifesaver in emergencies, but reckless use is financial quicksand.

Once you've built solid credit, loans and lower interest rates become accessible. Your credit score is your financial reputation—it tells lenders more about you than words ever could.

Some cards even offer perks like cash back or points. Use those wisely, channeling rewards into investments such as ETFs, REITs, or IRAs. Even $25 a month, compounded, can grow significantly over time. Redeem points for gift cards or store credits to save money. Build credit carefully, keep debt low, and you'll be positioned for financial growth.

Chapter 2: Wolf in Sheep's Clothing

Schools often told us they were teaching skills we'd need in the "real world." That was only half the truth. Once you actually step into adulthood, you quickly discover that the world revolves around money. Yes, education in literature, science, math, and everything else in between are valuable. If you want to become a doctor, engineer, or architect, you must master those fields. But for those who take a different path, the K–12 education is usually enough. What schools never taught us was financial freedom. The subject that had anything to do with money was math. Similar to math, both revolve around numbers and both follow a set of principles and formulas.

Humans, like any other creature, stay in familiar environments. To grow, you must leave that comfort zone and step into the unfamiliar. I remember classroom exercises where we were asked what we wanted to be when we grew up. Most kids gave safe answers—policeman, doctor, lawyer, firefighter, teacher. My first thought was different: I wanted to be a movie star or singer. At the time, I didn't dare write that down. I worried about being laughed at. That hesitation reflects how society often mocks people who think differently.

Later, I learned there were special schools for acting and performing and that some people worked their way into the industry or were discovered by scouts. Even back then, though, I was already thinking beyond the ordinary paycheck.

This is why I say K–12 education is essential but limited. Reading, writing, and other basic skills are crucial. Many people don't end up pursuing the career their degree prepared them for. Some earn a degree, try the job, hate it, and return to college for something else. What schools don't tell you is that most companies will happily pay for additional education if it benefits the business.

If your job requires certification, the company often covers it. I went through such process for the company I worked for. Why? Because investing in an existing employee who already knows the business is far cheaper than hiring someone new. If you like your job and want to advance, ask your manager. They may send you to classes or help fund training. Even if a promotion doesn't come immediately, you'll be ready when the opportunity arrives.

This is why I caution young people: don't rush into college without knowing what you really want. Unless you're absolutely sure, don't waste your time and money chasing a degree just because that's the "traditional path."

I worked at a restaurant for more than ten years as my first job. If I had known then what I know now, I could have begun my financial journey much earlier and maybe retired young like Warren Buffett. Back then, I'd heard of 401(k)s, IRAs, mutual funds, and index funds, but I wasn't curious enough to dive deeper. My restaurant job didn't offer benefits, and I didn't care because, like most people, I was addicted to the paycheck. I assumed that if something like a 401(k) were truly important, every job would offer it.

It wasn't until I got a retail job that I was first exposed to real benefits—401(k), healthcare, dental, vision. Even then, I didn't fully understand them. If you do nothing else with money, at least find a job that offers a 401(k) and start contributing early. Time is the most valuable resource in wealth-building. Don't make the same mistake as I did.

A 401(k) is available through an employer if you're a W-2 worker. For independent contractors (1099 workers), there are Solo 401(k) plans. The power of a 401(k) lies in its tax deferral—you contribute pre-tax income, lowering your taxable income now. Later, you pay taxes on withdrawals in retirement. Many employers also match a portion of your contributions, essentially giving you free money.

If you can't access a 401(k), open an Individual Retirement Account (IRA). There are two main types: Traditional and Roth. A Traditional IRA is tax-deferred—you pay taxes when you withdraw. A Roth IRA, popular with young people, allows after-tax contributions, but withdrawals later are tax-free. Think of it like planting a seed today and harvesting without tax later. Contribution limits and rules change every year, so always check current regulations.

In my twenties, I also experimented with CDs, bonds, and high-yield savings accounts. Banks pitched Certificates of Deposit (CDs) as if they were doing you a favor, but in truth, the terms favored the bank. You lend them your money for years at a modest interest rate, while they reinvest and loan it at much higher returns. The longer you locked in your money, the higher the interest is. You are essentially acting as a private lender, lending your money to the banks on their terms. Likewise, when the banks lend you money, they lend on their own terms as well. Whichever term you agreed to locked your money in for, you'll have to wait for its maturity date to withdraw the money without facing penalties.

Bonds work similarly, except you lend money to the government. There are various bonds you can buy; E- Bond and I-Bond are two of them. Each one has rules on how long you must leave it till it reaches its maturity date. Bonds are great tools to include in your tax saving strategy.

Later, I moved into high-yield savings accounts, I found some online banking paid far better than your average local banks. You can find decent rates at credit unions though. Online banks like GE Bank and Ally Bank offered higher interest, so I bounced my money back and forth depending on rates.

Eventually, I discovered index universal life insurance (IUL). Similar to whole life insurance, an IUL builds "cash value" that grows with the market. You can borrow against it; even use it to pay premiums once the value is high enough. And the death benefit is tax-free. Structured correctly, life insurance can be both protection and a wealth-building tool. With the right money education, it'll not only pass wealth onto your children, but to your grandchildren and thereafter.

At age 26, I also bought my first home, with city and government programs helping with the down payment. A home can be an asset, but only if it puts money in your pocket. Renting it out or using it for Airbnb can generate cash flow. Otherwise, as your primary residence, it becomes a liability—you pay the mortgage, insurance, and interest out of your pocket. Schools never explained amortization schedules, but I eventually learned that early mortgage payments go mostly toward interest, not principal. Over 30 years, you may pay double the house's value. Lenders know how to keep you locked in, often encouraging refinancing just to reset the interest clock. As you paid the mortgage over the years, your home accumulates equity. Equity is the current market value of your home minus the amount you have left. The four ways to access your home equity are cash-out refinance, equity loan, HELOC and to sell your home.

All of these financial tools—401(k), IRA, CDs, bonds, life insurance, and mortgages—can be useful. But whether they build wealth or keep you trapped depends on you.

It starts with your mindset. Are you contributing to an IRA just to save on taxes, or to build long-term wealth? Are you locking money into a CD simply for the advertised interest rate, or to protect your savings from economic swings? Are you buying a house only to live in it, or to create passive income?

What would you do if one million dollars landed in your hands today?

Chapter 3: Blue or Red Pill

Now comes the decision—blue pill or red pill. To decide means to "cut off" other options. If you decide on the blue pill, you remain in the life you already know, living in the programmed comfort of ignorant bliss. If you decide on the red pill, your eyes will be opened to opportunities that have always been there but were hidden by the conditioning that blocked your awareness. With the red pill, your mindset shifts, your vision clears, and your purpose strengthens. Change a person's mindset, change the person.

If you're still reading, I'm glad you've decided on the red pill and joined me on this journey. But before moving forward, let's revisit the wolf in sheep's clothing from Chapter 2. Many of the financial tools we're told to rely on—401(k)s, IRAs, CDs, savings accounts, and mortgages—are presented as desirable, while the fine print hides their flaws. Notice that I left life insurance off the list from the last sentence, for a reason.

401(k)
On the surface, a 401(k) looks like a smart choice. Many people contribute 10% or more of their paycheck, convinced they'll retire at 55 or 65 with a comfortable nest egg. While you can indeed build a sizeable retirement account this way, it's not the fastest route to financial independence.

The truth is, the 401(k) was never designed to be the sole source of retirement income. It was meant to be one leg of the "three-legged stool" retirement strategy alongside pensions and Social Security. But pensions are nearly extinct, and Social Security is uncertain. You can substitute any of the missing leg with your savings. Since pensions are rare to come by for the younger generations, dividends are the new pensions. Most employees don't explore alternatives because the 401(k) feels safe—and it's what everyone else does.

Companies that manage 401(k)s don't work for free. They earn money through hidden fees, employer contributions, and revenue-sharing with mutual fund companies. If your 401(k) is invested in dividend-paying stocks, those dividends often never reach you directly. A 401(k) isn't designed to make you rich—it's designed to keep you in the system. A wealthy employee is a customer lost.

IRA
An Individual Retirement Account (IRA) is like a savings account that invests your money in the stock market. Depending on your portfolio, it may include large-cap, mid-cap, small-cap, and international stocks. Dividends earned are reinvested automatically, compounding your returns.

Outside an IRA, if you built your own dividend-paying portfolio, you could choose to reinvest dividends (a DRIP plan) or take them as cash payouts. Inside an IRA, dividends are automatically reinvested, but the account comes with strict rules. Withdraw before age 59½, and you face penalties along with taxes.

IRAs are useful, but again, they're not the fastest way to reach financial freedom.

CDs and Savings Accounts
Were you aware that when you deposit money into CDs, savings, or even checking accounts, you are essentially lending your money to the bank? The bank takes your money, pools it with everyone else's, and reinvests it—while promising you a small return.

Banks make far more from your money than you'll ever see back. That's why many charge maintenance fees if you don't keep a minimum balance. They're not in the business of holding your money out of kindness—they're in business to profit from it.

You should only keep enough in savings for emergencies. Anything beyond that should be invested. Otherwise, inflation slowly eats away at your money's value. A CD promising 4% might look good, but after inflation (averaging 2% per year), your real return shrinks to 2%.

Bonds
For decades, governments have funded projects through bonds, paying citizens back with interest. While safe, bonds rarely outpace inflation or provide real wealth-building opportunities. It is used by the rich as a way to save on taxes and keep their money safe. It is safe knowing that the government is likely to print more money to ensure they can pay back the bonds.

Life Insurance
Life insurance agents often pitch policies as an investment vehicle. On the surface it may sound like an investment, but in truth it's not. It is a great place to put your extra money instead of putting it in your savings. When structured correctly, it can build cash value, which grows tax-deferred, with the potential to be tax-free. Money earned from interest in your savings account is taxed. Typically, if you withdraw from your cash value, you'll be taxed on the amount. If you take a loan against it, you won't get taxed. The cash value remains the same.

In my twenties, I bought into life insurance with the dream of one day living off its cash value. Properly funded, it can become a powerful wealth tool, but only if managed wisely. When you feel like you've built enough cash value, instead of borrowing money from the banks, you can borrow from your policy instead. You've become your own bank with better interest rates. It's very fascinating once you understand the power of borrowing your own money that you've been growing instead of borrowing from banks with high interest. Banks are afraid of this and love to keep this as a secret from you. Seek a specialist if you want to use life insurance as part of your wealth planning.

Real Estate
For years, I believed buying a home was the ultimate asset—until I read Robert Kiyosaki's Rich Dad Poor Dad. A home only becomes an asset when it puts money in your pocket. That means renting it out, not living in it. As a primary residence, your home is a liability. Mortgage payments, interest, insurance, and maintenance all take money out of your pocket.

The amortization schedule reveals how banks profit: in the early years of a mortgage, most of your payments go toward interest, not principal. Over 30 years, you often end up paying for the house twice. Lenders entice you to refinance with lower monthly payments, but refinancing resets the clock, keeping you in debt longer. Even "cash-out refinancing" eats away at the equity you've built. Another way to pay off your house is to roll it into a HELOC. HELOC stands for Home Equity Line of Credit. As a HELOC it's no longer a mortgage. Unlike a mortgage, a HELOC follows a simple interest schedule instead of an amortization schedule. A HELOC provides a revolving line of credit compared to a mortgage that has a non-revolving line of credit. The best part is that with the right strategy, you'll be able to pay off a 30 year loan within seven to ten years. I recommend checking out The Kwak Brothers on YouTube to learn more about HELOC.

The Bigger Picture
By now, you see the pattern. These traditional paths—401(k), IRA, CDs, bonds, mortgages—come with rules, penalties, and limitations. They aren't designed to make you financially free in your twenties or thirties. They're designed to keep you trading time for money until you're too old to enjoy it.

That's why you must choose wisely. Keep following the herd with the blue pill, or change your mindset, take the red pill, and step into financial awareness. Don't wait till you're near the end of your life to start enjoying life.

Chapter 4: Exodus

I reached a point where I told myself I wasn't going to keep waking up every morning just to grind until I was weak, wrinkled, and gray. The same feeling I had senior year—counting down to the day I could finally sleep in—came back stronger. I didn't want to "survive" anymore; I wanted to thrive. I believed there would come a day when we wouldn't worry about money, when my children would have a better life than I did. I might not come from a rich family, but my children and grandchildren will.

What does being rich and wealthy mean to you? To me, being rich means not just making one million dollars, but being worth one million dollars. Wealth is creating a legacy that will keep my family free of poverty for generations to come.

People say, "Health is the new wealth." There's truth in that, but here's another perspective: when you're struggling with money, stress and depression follow—and both wreck your health. As a wise man said, "You can buy a good doctor, but not good health." That's a good reminder that money isn't everything, but there are times when you wished you had money to solve everything. You may not think much about wealth while you're young and strong, but as you age, you'll wish you had the resources to tilt the odds back in your favor.

When I was sixteen, we cooked on a double cast-iron stove hooked to a single propane tank at the bottom of the basement stairs. My dad left, the mortgage was three months behind, and some mornings we woke to the electricity or water shut off—sometimes both. If only the power was out, we moved the food into a cooler with ice and boiled water to bathe. We cooked most meals on that propane stove. Eventually the house went into foreclosure. With help from the Housing Authority, we had two days to move what we could and leave the rest. We spent the next decade reacquiring what we'd lost. Those years reminded me there's nothing virtuous about being poor. I wish we'd had the money to solve our problems. Money doesn't change you—it amplifies who you already are.

I also learned why the rich rarely share what they know. The poor hand out advice; the rich are hesitant to. They understand that trying to help someone who isn't looking for change will only drain you and annoy them. You can test this by generously sharing information on social media. The wise will remain silent and the other half will turn it into a debate. Everyone experiences the world differently, and in their world, money "works" differently. When your message doesn't match their internal matrix, they reject it. That's why successful people would rather build wealth in silence than debate. Stop recycling the excuses that kept your grandparents, parents, and you stuck. Break the cycle. Don't "try"—commit. Tryouts expect failure; transformation requires devotion and consistency.

"Small minds talk about people, average minds talk about events, and great minds talk about ideas." You probably know someone in each the mindsets—and you've probably cycled through them yourself. But which one is your default mindset? Put a rich mindset next to a poor mindset and you'll get friction, resulting in frustration. Put like minds with like minds and you'll get agreement. The influences throughout your life—your uncle urging you to save for college, your dad telling you to spend like you have it, a mentor nudging you to invest—shape who you become.

We gravitate to people who share our values. I don't enjoy drinking, so I drift away from those who do. I can have a great time without alcohol. It's the same with money: your circle either fuels your future or anchors you to your past.

Rich people remove themselves from environments that don't serve them. If your circle keeps preaching that poverty is your destiny, you'll lose the will to overcome your circumstances. The best zero-dollar investment is your mindset. Feed it with books, podcasts, videos, and voices that talk about wealth. If you're surrounded by a poor mindset, build an escape plan—quietly. Don't announce your departure. Let your absence be the message. Be like a tree: first build deep roots in silence, then break through the soil when you're strong enough to withstand the wind. Work in the dark; let results reveal you.

There will always be those who despise and love you regardless if you're poor or rich. People will come and go out of your life. Some will stick with you through it all. Just like your friends from high school whom you thought will always be part of your life after high school. Everyone went on to pursue their own goals, creating distance between the bonds you guys once had.

Don't pour energy into people who don't share your goals. They'll hand you reasons "why it won't work" and try to re-educate you back into the herd. Help those who want help; let the rest be. When should you be generous with your knowledge? In front of an audience that has paid— with money or with their attention. Free samples are fine, but value sticks when there's buy-in. If someone waits until you're successful to ask for "general advice," you can give a little for free and charge for the best kept secrets—not because you're arrogant, but because people will value what they invest in.

The Bible is rich with business principles if you have the open mind to see them. I learned many through Myron Golden, a business consultant who teaches from a biblical perspective. Consider Abram whom later became Abraham. Abram was reminded everyday by the people who knew him of the shame and lack that he carried. God told him to leave his country, his people, his father's house, and go to the land he would be shown. There, Abram became more than he was—greater and wealthier. The lesson: you must leave the familiar to become who you're meant to be.

It's the same story played out in modern life. A musician leaves a small town for a bigger stage. An actor gives up old routines for Hollywood. An employee relocates for a promotion. Growth lives beyond your comfort zone. Refuse to move, refuse to grow.

Think of Moses leading his people out of bondage. An eleven-day journey became forty years because of doubt, division, and old mindsets. Are you postponing your financial education even though you know it's missing? Are you clinging to the comfort of the known? Remember your first job—how unfamiliar it felt—yet you pushed through because adulthood required it. A job offers predictable pay and a sense of safety. There's nothing wrong with that if it's where you want to stay. But the road to a better place might be one book, one video, one mentor away. Start anywhere—but start. The first step of the journey is taking the first step.

As your financial life grows, so will your circle. You'll find yourself around people with deep expertise: an attorney, CPA, tax strategist, bookkeeper, coach, property manager. Some friends and family will drift away; the ones who truly believe in you will remain.

When you're ready to leave where you are—mentally or physically—do it in silence. Don't announce it. Some will try to sabotage your conviction. Let your progress speak. Build your wealth like a tree builds roots: quietly, consistently, out of sight. Then let your actions and results reveal you to the world.

Chapter 5: Breakthrough

There were three moments that changed my financial outlook, each one bigger than the last.

First, the 2020 pandemic; I'd known about Robinhood for years but never bothered. Quarantine gave me time, so I opened an account and bought a few stocks. When Dogecoin went viral, some of my family and I jumped in around 13 cents, planning to hold and sell on the next pop. I didn't think of myself as an investor then—I was just buying and hoping. Looking back, I was an investor without the education. I stumbled across the terms "diamond hands" and "paper hands". Having diamond hands is when you ignore the noises and fear when the market appears to be on the decline. You don't sell out of panic and hold onto your assets. When you panic and sell out of fear, this is called having paper hands. If I was aware that they allow you to buy portions of crypto and stocks during that time, I would've bought a good share of Bitcoin. Like anything, there's always risk. I lost money and learned lessons along the way. Every rich person will tell you they've lost money at some point —it's part of the process. There's a difference between losing money and going broke.

Second, I listened to Robert Kiyosaki's Rich Dad Poor Dad audio book. My day job allowed me to learn while I worked, because I got bored of music and podcasts. Instead of entertaining myself, I was educating myself. That book reframed everything—assets vs. liabilities, poor mindset vs. rich mindset, cash flow, passive income. I started connecting the dots between my past decisions and my results. I've been collecting various collectibles over the years, waiting to sell them when their price rises. I realized I hadn't been building assets; I'd been stacking inventory—things that only pay you once when you sell them. Worst, those collectibles have not been putting money into my pocket over the years. Assets, by contrast, pay you repeatedly while you still own the asset. For example, a rental home pays you monthly without you needing to sell it. Dividend stocks and ETFs pay you repeatedly while you hold onto them.

I also listened to Kiyosaki's Why "A" Students Work for "C" Students and "B" Students Work for the Government. "A" students are the academic achievers; they work for the "C" students. "B" students are the bureaucrats that work in government roles. The geniuses during our time weren't 4.0 GPA students or the smartest academically; still they changed the world with their creativity. A key lesson from the book: a paycheck feels safe, so people get addicted to it and never build other income streams. The real world doesn't care about your academic grades; it cares about your credit score, your cash flow, and your ability to repay. When you get a loan, banks don't care about your grades, they care about how much money you have. Degrees can help you get a decent paying job, but financial literacy helps set you free. When you're able to market yourself well to the world, many will value and seek you.

Third, I opened an Acorns account—initially just out of curiosity. I knew Acorns rounded up your purchases and saves the difference in an account for you. I found out that it offered other services such as banking and investment options.

One day I noticed a transaction in my investment portfolio labeled: dividends. That one word flipped a switch. I dug in and learned my Acorns investment portfolio invested in ETFs like VOO, IJH, IJR, and IXUS—and that dividends were being paid and reinvested. I asked myself how I can get more, so I went looking for more. I learned that ETFs, REITs, and some individual stocks pay on different schedules—yearly, quarterly, monthly, even weekly (though weekly can be inconsistent). In Acorns, you can choose individual holdings for up to 50% of your investment portfolio; not every ticker is available though. Quarterly dividends seem to be the most popular. There are two ETF I found on Acorns; JPMorgan Equity Premium Income (JEPI) and Bitcoin's ETF (BITO) that pays monthly. BITO gives investors the opportunity to invest in Bitcoin without actually owning any Bitcoin. These two ETF in Acorns will give you a nice return on investment (ROI).

You can find videos online that love Acorns and videos that don't. That's fine. I recommend it for beginners who want to start investing, build habits, and see dividends in action. When you understand how it all works, you can pass it along to friends and family who are seeking financial change. Help the people who want help; let the rest be.

Before Acorns, I'd been shopping for life insurance with the goal of building cash value. I spoke with a local agent—call him Jack—who tried to steer me toward budgeting and saving after sharing that I wanted to build a financial future with cash value inside a life policy. That wasn't what I wanted at the time, so I stopped taking his calls. This experience helped me understand that when a person's mindset is not in the right place to welcome help, there is nothing you can do or say. You can tell a person the steps to becoming rich, but unless they become the person that will take those steps, they will not act on it. If it was that easy, everyone would've been doing it. I kept thinking back to Jack that maybe he would've introduced me to the world of investing if I stuck with him a bit longer, but now we'll know.

As I continued my financial education, YouTube introduced me to Myron Golden, author of From the Trash Man to the Cash Man and B.O.S.S. Moves. His first video I watched was about why people can't sell. He teaches business through a biblical lens, and it clicked. If what you've been doing for a decade hasn't changed your life, perhaps try something new. From him I learned principles I'll keep forever.

One lesson I learned from Myron Golden is that, don't be afraid to get rejected when making sales. Instead of looking for people to sell to, make yourself discoverable to those that already desire what you offer. Thousands to millions of people are already looking for what you have to sell; they'll happily hand over the money if only they knew how to find you. You need to have the desire to help others more than you yourself. People can tell when you are being genuine or if you're in it for yourself. Help people by actually helping them. Getting denied is part of the growing process. Don't get discouraged if you don't make a sell, presentation after presentation. Eventually you'll get good to the point where people can't resist saying "yes.

One of Myron's frameworks is the four levels of value we use to create income:

Implementation — trading muscle and time for money. Since muscle and time are limited resources, your income is capped around $90k annually on the high end.

Unification — any management role. When you are in charge of people to get the task done, you step into the low six figures. Low end of $60k to high end of $300K.

Communication — using your communication skills or mouth to make money. A broad range of options from singing, acting, coaching, interviewing people, podcast, and streaming. When you use your communication skills to move the masses, you can expect to make a few millions dollars on the high end.

Imagination — the highest level of value; using your mind to make money. You can expect anything from millions to billions. Take all the technology that changed the way we live today. The smartphone for example; started in someone's mind, they imagined it, and then used their communication skills along with unification to implement it into reality.

You might notice that the different levels of value can be combined.

Another framework: the three places people derive value, which predicts where they'll put their money:

- Past perceived void — you lacked something growing up (nice shoes, status, and comfort), so you spend to fill that gap.
- Present perceived value — what you value now (education, gear, experiences), that's where your money will go.
- Future perceived value — what you believe will have value later (health, investments, gold/silver, training) will attract your investment.

If you can appeal to any of the three places that a person draws their values from, you can easily figure out how to help them.

In the end, my "breakthrough" wasn't a single trade or a lottery ticket. It was a sequence:

- Start anywhere (Robinhood, a first dividend, a single ETF).
- Educate your mindset (books, audiobooks, mentors).
- Build systems (automations, consistent contributions).
- Accumulate assets that pay you—on a schedule you can count on.

That's when things start to compound—not just your money, but your identity. You stop being someone who hopes and start being someone who builds.

Chapter 6: Philosophy of Money

Either you're making someone else rich, or someone else is making you rich. Like energy and matter that change form, money constantly changes hands—it never disappears. It simply flows from one pocket to another.

Money doesn't discriminate. It doesn't care about your skin color, your values, your family history, your school grades, or anything that you made yourself believed. Money goes to those who welcome it.

If you've ever said, "I can't be rich because of my circumstances," then ask yourself: what have you done to change them? The solution isn't just working more jobs or collecting more degrees. Those things may help for a time, but they don't fix the root problem. True change begins within.

How many people do you know with multiple jobs or multiple degrees who are still struggling—still stuck in the rat race? You'll never become who you want to be until you first change the way you think.

It's a common misconception that "money is the root of all evil." People often use this excuse to justify staying broke.

The same kind of reasoning gets used when people say guns kill people or video games promote violence. But history proves otherwise—humans were killing long before guns were invented and violence been around long before video games. Unless money or guns suddenly grow arms, legs, and brains, they remain nothing more than tools.

It isn't money that corrupts—it's the love of money. If you despise the rich, or despise money itself, you'll never become what you despise. People rarely go out of their way to become what they hate.

The truth is, both good people and bad people have the same opportunities to build wealth. Nothing stops either group from doing so. Yet often, "good" people are the quickest to preach that wealthy people are evil—while doing nothing themselves to rewrite the story. If you believe all rich people are corrupt, but never step into wealth to prove otherwise, then the narrative never changes.

Think about the last time you heard of a wealthy person robbing a convenience store, holding up a bank, or committing petty theft for loose change.

Who is more likely to rob a gas station—the poor man desperate for a few dollars, or the wealthy man who already has more than enough?

Who is more likely to scam you out of your savings—the person drowning in debt, or the one already financially secure?

Money doesn't change you—it reveals you. It magnifies what's already in your heart.

If you are generous, money gives you the ability to give more. If you are greedy, money gives you the ability to hoard more.

That's why people often say, "Money made him this way." The truth is, money simply gave him the freedom to express what was already inside.

Another common misconception is that the rich don't pay taxes—that they commit tax evasion and are simply greedy. Let's think about that for a moment. How do you legally reduce taxes? The IRS publishes a tax code that spells out how to save on taxes. You can simply go to the IRS website and learn the rules of the game. It's a rulebook that explains credits and deductions—and like any game, if you want to win, learn the rules and use them to your advantage.

Two well-known ways to lower taxes are real estate and charitable giving. Ask yourself: who typically gives the largest donations to nonprofits—someone working a 9–5 with limited income, or someone with thousands or millions in capital? When was the last time you personally gave a significant portion of your income to a cause—enough to meaningfully move the needle for that organization on your own?

Many wealthy people give substantial amounts quietly, while most of us send a portion of every paycheck to the government through taxes. By following the IRS rulebook, many wealthy people legally pay very little in taxes. Because schools rarely teach this, we're quick to conclude that "the rich don't pay taxes" or "they should be taxed more." Meanwhile, the typical W-2 employee often ends up paying more tax than people who understand and apply the rules. The common person gets taxed at the federal level, state level, local level (shopping at stores), and FICA. While the rich can minimize or eliminate being tax by understanding the tax code.

Money isn't good or bad—it's neutral. It only does what you tell it to do. Money is a servant to your commands.

- If you want it to go to waste, it will.
- If you want it to multiply, it will.

A poor mindset sees money only as something to spend. A wealthy mindset sees money as something to grow.

- The poor ask: "What can I buy with this?"
- The rich ask: "How can I multiply this?"

Money doesn't care which path you choose. It simply obeys the mindset that controls it.

There's a theory that if all the money in the world were distributed equally, within a few short years the money would end up right back in the same hands it originally came from.

Why? Because money in the hands of someone who doesn't know how to manage it will always disappear.

- Give money to a gambler, and they'll gamble it away.
- Give money to a drug addict, and they'll spend it on drugs.
- Give money to an alcoholic, and they'll drink it away.
- Give money to someone financially illiterate, and they'll blow it on liabilities—flashy cars, clothes, and temporary luxuries.

- Give money to a saver, and they'll just save it. Money loses value over time due to inflation.

We often believe that having more money will solve our problems. Truth is, when we get more money, we tend to spend more. On the other hand, give that same money to someone who understands how money works, and they'll use it to buy assets, investments, and cash-flowing opportunities.

Eventually, the cycle resets. The money flows back to those who know how to manage it.

This is why the poor often stay poor and the rich grow richer. It isn't always because of greed or corruption. More often, it's because of knowledge and discipline. Financial literacy creates separation.

You can hand two people the exact same amount of money, and in ten years one will be broke while the other is financially free. The difference isn't luck—it's mindset and education.

The lesson of giving a man a fish and he eats for one day, teach him how to fish and he'll feed himself indefinitely. This is an important lesson that can be applied to many aspects in life; it's no different when it comes to money.

Give someone some cash and they'll keep it for a short time. Teach them how to get it and grow money, and they'll have endless streams of income indefinitely. If someone gives you a million dollars, you've become a millionaire. But if you want to stay a millionaire, you'd better find a way to keep that million. Losing even one cent strips you of the title.

A common answer when asking people how much money they would like to have is, "not too much." Somewhere along the way, we were taught to believe that having too much money or wealth is not virtuous. Too much wealth gets labeled as greed—like you're hoarding it while others go without. If you think this way, have you ventured outside of your day job in search of wealth and found that there is less or are you just thinking there is less because you've not seen any of the wealth come your way? The idea that wealth works like a pie — where the more one person takes, the less there is left for others — presets a false limitation on your imagination. There is an abundance of wealth all around you; you just lack the awareness to see it.

If you feel that the rich should share their wealth to the world and help the poor instead of hoarding it; what's stopping you from accumulating wealth and be the one that shares it with the rest of the world. Instead you want to use other people's money towards your cause, but you don't care enough to get the money yourself for your own cause.

We want our children to get the highest education as possible, be as smart as possible, we want to be as healthy as we can, live as long as we can, and the list goes on. In every other aspects of our life, we want to have as much as possible; somehow when it comes to money, we are afraid.

Ask yourself this: if you woke up tomorrow a multi-millionaire, would you feel any less virtuous or less humble? Would you suddenly have evil intentions? Wealth is power, and like any form of power, it only amplifies who you are inside.

That's why I love to reference Marvel's Captain America: The First Avenger. Steve Rogers was chosen to undergo the super-soldier serum because of his good heart and nature, as observed by the doctor. Steve was the kind of man who stood up to a bigger bully at the theater and threw himself on a grenade during training to shield his comrades. The doctor saw that Rogers had a pure heart. When the doctor was dying from a gunshot wound, he reminded Steve not to forget why he was chosen, pointing to his chest where his heart was. To me, this gesture meant: "Use it for good, Steve. Use it for good."

Later, in the TV series, John Walker became America's choice for the next Captain America. He also received the serum, but unlike Steve, he was quick to anger, letting his emotions override his judgment. That led to him murdering a foreign national in public. The lesson? Any form of power only amplifies who you really are inside.

Someone having an abundance of wealth doesn't mean there's less out there. It's not like if someone takes a large piece of pie, there's less pie left for you. Consider this: your million dollars might be sitting in someone else's pocket right now. Offer them something of value, and they'll happily hand the money over.

We see this every day. A restaurant offers food to customers. Food is valuable because you need to eat. In exchange for being fed, you hand them your money. Or maybe you provide a service like video editing—someone values your skill, and in return, they pay you.

You might create a life-changing gadget like the next iPhone. Get the world to believe your gadget is an everyday necessity, and people will pay whatever price you set. Or you might create an app that makes tasks easier. Make it available to the masses through the App Store or Google Play, and money will flow your way. Even a simple game like Flappy Bird made its creator millions.

Or consider entertainment. You create content and upload it to YouTube. People pay with their attention, and YouTube pays you. The options are endless. Think like this; if a billion people each gave you a dollar, you'd be a billionaire.

Believing that having too much money automatically equals evil will keep you from becoming rich. Replace evil with virtuous. Having too much money and being virtuous can go together too.

You've probably thought that if one day you became rich, you'll help those in need. I'll offer you this thought; when you do become wealthy, you will realized that the work and mindset you had to go through, anybody is able go through the same process, as a result of this revelation, you'll withdraw from your initial thought. By giving a person free money, you are stripping them of the growth they could've achieved if you haven't given them the money. It wouldn't be fair to them. Money will come and go, but knowledge stays forever. If everyone wanted to become rich as bad as they wanted to graduate high school, they'll find a way like they did in high school.

At any level of wealth, you'll want to protect it. There will always be those who try to steal what you've built. You'll also have people come into your life asking for money. What you can offer that's more valuable than money itself is the knowledge of how to obtain it for themselves.

We often ask: "Why don't the rich just give money to the needy?" The rich don't hand out money in the same way most of us don't give money to every person we see holding a sign at the corner of Wal-Mart. The wealthy know we all have the same opportunity to become rich—just like we know that the person on the corner has the same opportunity to get a job. The rich are treating us the same way we treat the homeless, and yet, we get mad at them for it. Some choose to stay homeless, some choose to remain poor, and some chose to become rich.

In today's economy, it's a choice: work hard, putting in time and strenuous labor for a little bit of someone else's money, or learn to build wealth yourself.

I've known people who rely on government programs. Some do their best to stay on those programs. Instead of striving to make thousands or even millions, they'd rather keep doing what they've been doing for less, waiting for a couple hundred dollars from the government. They're afraid to make more money in fear of losing benefits if their income exceeds the limits. That mindset gets passed down to their children and beyond, unless.

I've been on government programs myself. I'm not saying they aren't necessary or that I wasn't thankful—I was. But my goal was never to remain there for life. Someone once said that if you're middle class, it's easier to be in lower class. Having lived in the lower class for much of my life, I can confirm—it's a chore.

The energy and time spent digging for proof of income and other documents when applying for programs could have been used instead to learn new skills and build wealth. When we finally no longer qualified for food stamps, energy assistance, or government health insurance, I knew we were doing something right. It meant no more digging for paperwork, no more chasing family members for pay stubs, no more re-certification appointments, and no more proving we were struggling. Fewer chores meant more time for the things I love.

I've also been in conversations where someone would explain how hard life is for them to build wealth or invest due to their circumstances. I could have shared my story too, but then it would just be a contest over who is more miserable. While the rich compete to scale businesses, the poor often compete in the opposite direction—a race to the bottom. Instead of sharing misery, we should be sharing strategies to better our lives. That way, we can compete in a race to the top.

Three of the most common reasons people don't invest are:
1. I don't have money for it.
2. I don't know where to start.
3. I lack financial education.

When people think about investing, they often believe it requires a large sum of money or that they have to be rich to start. That's true for some opportunities, but not all. I once had someone scold me for "investing while letting my family starve." In his mind, he thought I was putting all my money into investments while neglecting bills, food, and clothing. Maybe he only knew about investment options that required big minimum deposits—or he was just quick to judge. I explained that you can start with as little as $20 and build from there.

I budgeted on a 75/15/10 plan: 10% of my income went to an emergency fund, 15% into investments, and 75% for everything else. We even kept our grocery budget to around $300 a month (adjusting for inflation). I shared with him that you don't need much to start in the stock market or crypto—you can buy fractional shares. The scolding turned into wishing me luck in hopes that I don't lose all my money when the stock market falls.

That fear is common. People see the stock market in the red and panic, fearing they'll lose everything. In response, they pull out and take the loss. But you don't lose until you sell. Given time, markets rebound, and you'll recover—or profit.

Ironically, many people are scared to invest but have no problem gambling their money away. They'll drop $10 on a lottery ticket or $1,000 at a casino with zero expectation of getting any of it back if they lose. Investing, by contrast, carries a far greater chance of return. Yet people will gamble on chance rather than invest in growth.

We live in a fast-food, microwave culture where everyone wants results instantly. People want to get rich quick while running from anything labeled a "get rich quick scheme." Personally, I'm open to one—because as Myron Golden put it: "The opposite of a get rich quick scheme is staying poor for the rest of your life scheme." At the end of the day, it all comes down to education—and miseducation.

I was once one of those who didn't know where to start investing. I hadn't been exposed to that world, so I couldn't even picture what the first step looked like. Do I go to a bank? Who do I ask? What do I need to do? Those are fair questions. Today, the internet and AI make those answers available instantly. A single Google search can suggest top investment options. AI can be your personal finance assistance and tell you everything you want to know.

Another option is if you know someone doing better than you, talk to them. Listen to money podcasts. Pick up a finance book. I started with Rich Dad Poor Dad. It was a good first step that led to more. As Myron Golden said "A book that can't help you is a book you don't read." Information is more abundant and accessible today than ever before. There's no excuse not to start.

Have you presented an idea to someone, they often say they don't know how, or they don't have the skills? Tell someone they'd make a good streamer or podcaster, and they'll list reasons why they can't: they've never used a camera, don't know how to edit, never done it before, so they won't try. Tell someone they'd be good in real estate, and they'll explain why they can't. Excuses stack up quickly.

But my philosophy is this: if you wait until you have all the skills, knowledge, approval of others, money, or time, by the time you do, someone else will have already gotten there first; it'll be too late for you. Programmers weren't born knowing how to code. Doctors weren't born knowing how to treat patients. Best-selling authors weren't born knowing how to write best-sellers. Everyone who makes millions from their skills had to start from zero.

If you're waiting to wake up one day suddenly knowing how to make millions, it will never come. Imagine if Bill Gates or Elon Musk had waited until they were "ready." Someone else would've beaten them to it first.

Have you ever had the answer to something, but someone else raised their hand first and gave the answer because you procrastinated? They get all the glory, and you're left wondering: "what if?"

Chapter 7 – Reflection

Looking back, I wish I would've done it sooner. Time is the most valuable currency that we can't get more of. We've been taught that time is money. As a result, we trade our time for money. The rich value time more than money. You can always get more money, but you can't get more time. I reflect from time to time the benefits I would've gotten if I had started in my early twenties. Instead, like the majority, I was taught to get a job and climb the corporate ladder to make more money. I didn't realize I chose the hard way to make money and didn't optimize my money.

I will leave you with these few thoughts. If you have the funds to start a business, what business would you start? The most common businesses I've seen within my community are running a store or a restaurant. At one point in my life, that's what I thought I was going to do if I ever started my own business. Then I got exposed to other business ideas. I asked myself, what businesses create passive income rather than being another job?

When the words "passive income" is brought up, real estate is always in the conversation. Owning real estate, renting it to tenants, and collecting monthly rent is a form of passive income. Running a restaurant or a store where you have to be there to run it—that's not passive, that's buying yourself a job. Unless you can afford to hire a manager and employees to run the restaurant or store for you, you are the manager and employee. I wouldn't want a business where I have to wake up every morning to open the doors, set everything up, be there all day, and close up shop at night. That's the same as having a normal day job. You'll find that you'll be stuck working more and harder than if you were working for someone else. When you aren't there, money isn't coming in. How about a business that can run itself without you being there? Even when you're not around, money still comes in. If you enjoy cooking or customer service, plenty of jobs already provide that experience. Don't create or buy a business that only adds more responsibility —unless that's truly what you want.

Automatic Carwash

An example of a business that can run itself without you being there is an automatic carwash. Not the kind where someone needs to be there, but one that is fully automated. At an automatic carwash, the customer pays, the door opens, they drive in, and they come out with a clean car. An automatic carwash runs itself, even while you're sleeping.

There's one near my residence that happens to be my favorite. I go there every time my car needs washing. Many times I've seen five or six cars lined up. While waiting in line, I realized the owner just made close to a hundred dollars within the thirty minutes I was there. The owner could've been on vacation anywhere in the world while his carwash was making him money. Of course, it will require maintenance and repairs, but don't let that scare you. It's no different than anything else that needs regular maintenance. It's like housekeeping: a store owner sweeping the floor or facing the shelves to keep things in order.

Storage Units

Another business idea that requires little hands-on work or presence is a storage unit. In today's world, you can set up an online system where you never have to meet the customer. They can rent and pay online. Think of renting storage units like renting out a house—but instead, the house is for their belongings to live in.

They pay you monthly rent, just like tenants pay landlords. If they fail to pay within the legal grace period, they lose access to the unit and you can auction it off. The rental fee for each unit can vary depending on demand. For example, if you only have one unit left to rent, you can charge more than you did for the first few units. It's simply supply and demand. Yes, you'll need to make repairs and replace equipment along the way, but that is normal for any business.

Laundromats

When you go to a laundromat, some may have staff present, but many are fully self-serve. A laundromat with only washers and dryers, no dry cleaning or other services, saves on labor costs. Other than opening and closing the doors, it requires little of your presence.

You'll have to do some housekeeping and collect your money, but you can make it as passive as you want. Installing card readers can eliminate the hassle of coin machines. Of course, you never know what kind of customers you'll get. Some will respect your equipment, while others will abuse it. Some will use the machines properly, while others will shove random objects inside. Some customers may cost you more in repairs than you'd like. But overall, laundromats are another business idea that can mostly run itself without demanding all of your time.

Real Estate

Real estate is a favorite among those who want to create passive income. If you don't want to do any other option, real estate has proven time and time again as a way to build passive income. The reason so many people turn to real estate is because it offers some of the best tax benefits in the entire tax code.

Aside from taxes, it's easy to understand: you rent out a home to tenants, they pay you monthly rent. If your mortgage is $1,500 and you charge $2,000, you pocket $500 each month. Repeat this with more homes and your passive income grows. On top of that, your tenants are paying down your mortgage while you build equity.

Words Are a Powerful Tool

Words are a powerful tool. Whether you're looking at it spiritually or practically, words play an impactful role in who we are.

We were taught to use encouraging words, positive words, winning words, in other parts of our lives, but left out wealth and money. It's believed that money comes to those who fill their lives with words of prosperity; it avoids those who fill their lives with words of poverty.

The words you use reveal where you are in your financial journey. Saying "How can I afford this?" versus "I can't afford this" creates two very different mindsets. Someone who says, "That's too expensive," versus someone who isn't bothered by the price tells two different stories. There are words the rich stop using because they are no longer true in their world. There are words the poor keep using, which keep them stuck; unless.

They can be called "rich words" and "poor words." Saying you're hungry or starving may be just an expression, but money can't tell the difference between an expression and a spoken truth. When you think of the words hungry and starving, does the picture of a well fed person like you and I come into mind or does the picture of an actual hungry starving child you've seen on social media come to mind? If you were to Google hungry and starving, what do you expect to find? When you say you are hungry, you are using a word that a person less fortunate than you are would use; and can only use because there is no other words they can use to describe the state that they're in. If you know when your next meal is going to be; you're simply eating again because it's that time. You can also say that you're craving for some food, similar to drinking water when you feel thirsty. You wouldn't wait till you're dehydrated to drink water. Likewise, you wouldn't wait till you're starving to eat. Your body tells you when it's time to drink more water and when to eat before you put it in a critical state. If a well fed nourished person is feeling hungry on a daily basis, then how do we describe those that are less fortunate? Saying you're hungry when you were having three meals a day is a misrepresentation.

About a Team Using Encouraging Words

When it comes to the power of words, you wouldn't hear a team that's aiming to win say, "We are weak! We can't do it! We aren't the best!" If you want to win at life, saying things like, "I'm broke, I'm poor, I can't do it, I can't become rich," will never put you in the winning mindset.

Would you go to a job interview thinking you won't get the job? No—you would go in optimistic, doing your best, believing you'll land it. When it comes to wealth, why should it be any different? Through the use of words, we shape our reality.

When the Stock Market Falls

When the stock market falls, will you panic in fear or will you see it as an opportunity?

I remember a coworker once expressing concern about our company's stock falling during a recession. I explained to him that you still get paid a dividend. You don't lose money unless you sell. The market always rebounds.

Would you save your money, or would you invest it? Where a person puts their money reveals where their values lie. Someone talking about going to college to climb the corporate ladder is on a slow path to millions. Someone talking about an idea that could make millions is aiming for the faster path. The poor and the rich use very different vocabularies. What vocabularies are in your dictionary?

Seeking Help From an Outside Force

Do you ever feel like doing isn't enough? That maybe you need help from an outside force—whether unseen, spiritual, or just luck?

Think of it like a video game: everyone is born with a certain amount of luck points. Some have more than others. In a video game, if you're low on luck, you can equip charms and accessories to boost it. If you're born rich, you're very lucky—but you may lack the knowledge to maintain it and risk losing it all. If you're born with a strong physique but lack intelligence or luck, you work to build what you lack.

Some people believe in boosting their luck with something like Feng Shui. Feng Shui comes from Chinese geomancy. It's a spiritual approach that teaches how to attract wealth into your home by placing certain things in specific areas. Feng Shui isn't just about money—it can also focus on relationships, careers, and health. I started noticing Feng Shui signs everywhere in Chinese restaurants once I learned about it. Subtle signs of Feng Shui in a business setting are lucky bamboo sitting by the cashier counter, a Maneki Neko lucky cat by the entrance, and indoor plants placed around the setting. Whether you believe in it or not, the lesson is to be open to outside help and methods that may improve your life. Every culture has its own similar belief system. Whichever you choose, don't make it the primary driving force, but have it as a supplement.

Water

Water is a sign of wealth, it brings wealth. Many cities and countries that have prospered or are prospering are connected to some body of water. Water brings opportunities such as trading, access to resources and water is a life sustaining element. Take the three countries of Laos, Thailand and Vietnam. Thailand and Vietnam have large body of water touching them, while Laos is stuck in the middle, cut off from large body of water; landlocked. Do you remember buying any products that are from Laos? You mainly see products from Thailand and Vietnam in the Oriental aisle. Thailand and Vietnam are both ahead of Laos economically.

China makes the world go round, no surprise since its east coast touches a large body of water. On a smaller scale, some of the states like Florida, California and New York are thriving with people and opportunities due to their location. On a micro level you've probably seen cities, towns, villages thriving better than others due to having a body of water such as a lake or river running through or near them. All of this is known as geography if you're looking at it from a scientific point of view. I've taken the Feng Shui approach with favorable results. Some are born with an abundance of luck that they don't need help from any outside influence. Some go through life relying solely on fate. Some only believe in science; either way is ok. Do what works for you.

Living in an Era Where You're Born Poor but Can Die Rich

We live in an era where if you're born poor, you can become rich and die rich.

Back in the agricultural era, land equaled wealth. If your family owned land, you were rich. You remain rich until someone comes and takes it away. If you were born poor, you were poor for life. Today, wealth isn't only tied to land. It's tied to creativity, knowledge, and technology.

The "land" of today sits in the palm of your hands—your phone. Your phone is like an ATM connected to the world bank. With it, people in the world can send money straight to your phone. Let me explain; you don't need fancy equipment to post a video on YouTube; you can just use your phone. People use their phones to earn on TikTok and Instagram. You can use your phone to close a deal; shortly after, the money will appear on your phone.

Do you love singing? Record yourself on your phone, grow an audience, and you could make millions. Do you feel photogenic? Use your phone to reach the masses and build a following. Wealth is everywhere—you just have to see it.

About Watching a Show

Have you ever watched a show, movie, or read a book that sparked ideas of your own? Maybe you thought, "If I was the author, I would've done it better."

That's your creative drive telling you something. Every big franchise—Harry Potter, Twilight, Dragon Ball—started with one person's idea. Jeff Bezos was one idea away from Amazon, Elon Musk was one idea away from creating Tesla, and the list goes on. They were one idea away; you are one idea away from your breakthrough.

Becoming an author is easier than ever. You don't have to go the traditional route—there are online publishers; you can be a self-publisher. It doesn't have to be fantasy novel like Harry Potter. You can write about what you know; derive from your personal experiences. Even something like how to be the best employee could become a book. There are millions of fabulous employees, but there aren't millions of books on the subject. Every year, there are millions of young adults fresh out of high school looking for guidance on how to stand out. Don't keep your knowledge locked up. Share it, teach it, and monetize it.

The Trap of Waiting for a Raise

When raises come, you'll get somewhere between a dollar and three dollars. At first, it feels satisfying—you think you can finally buy that thing you've been putting off. But the ugly reality is, while you got a two-dollar raise, eggs also went up by two dollars, some maybe more.

In truth, pay raises rarely keep up with inflation. If you're getting less than a dollar raise, you're actually falling behind. If you stay on that path, you'll keep falling further behind. Waiting for raises is not a wealth strategy.

If You're Good at Something

What if I told you that if you're good at something—or you have a certain skill set—you can make more money not by doing it, but by teaching it or entertaining with it.

Take sports, for example. If you're good at basketball, you entertain people by playing. If you're great at guitar, you can make more money teaching others how to play than just performing.

You can teach one-on-one in person, or you teach thousands online with videos and courses. If you're a nail tech, you could make tutorials and teach others instead of only working on one client at a time. A video can reach thousands in the same time it would take you to serve one customer. You create the content once, and get paid repeatedly for it. If you just stick to doing the job, you'll always have to be present. But if you teach or entertain, you multiply your income.

The Two Statements

There are two statements to consider and apply to your life:
- "I can't be rich because I have you guys."
- "I have to become rich because I have you guys."

These refer to having children, but you can change it up to fit your situation. Some people see kids as an obstacle. Others see them as the reason they must succeed. Life is full of obstacles, but you get to decide whether they stop you or motivate you.

When you turned eighteen, you became an adult. You lose the right to complain. If you don't like something, change it. Don't sit around blaming circumstances or others—it will not change or make it better. Even in politics, if you don't like what's happening, vote. In money, "vote" with how you spend. Put your money where it will change your life.

No Matter How Much Money You Make

Remember that no matter how much money you make, by strategically deploying your money, you can build wealth. The goal is not to look rich, but to be rich. It's not about how much you make, but how you spend it, and how much you keep.

There are people making six figures who are struggling just like the poor. Some are living paycheck to paycheck because every time they get paid, the money is already spent before it even hits their account. They buy the new car, the bigger house, the newest gadgets, clothes, and vacations—all to look like they're rich. But in reality, they're broke with fancy things.

There is a difference between making $100,000 in a year and being worth $100,000. Income is not wealth. Wealth is what you keep, what you grow, and what you own.

A person making $50K a year who invests, saves, and builds assets can end up wealthier than someone making $150K a year who spends it all to "look rich." Showing off fancy things proves how much money you spent, not how much money you own.

Every dollar should have a job—save, invest, pay down debt, give, and enjoy in that order. Put your money to work so that money works for you.

Looking rich feeds the ego. Being rich feeds the future. The next ten years are going to come regardless if you start or not. If you don't start, ten years from now you will look back with regret, stuck in the same place. If you do start, ten years from now, you'll thank yourself.

Looking back, I wish I would've started sooner. That's the lesson. The best time to start was yesterday. The next best time is today. Best to start now.

www.ingramcontent.com/pod-product-compliance
Lightning Source LLC
LaVergne TN
LVHW010437070526
838199LV00066B/6064